MW01531365

Quit Sitting Around on Your Ashes

11/1/2010

Jennie Bible

Quit Sitting Around on Your Ashes

ISBN 9781453856390

Copyright © 2010 by Jennie Bible

925 Willow

Chelsea, OK 74016

Email: jenniebible@sbcglobal.net

Cover photograph by Jennie Bible,

Copyright © 2009 by Jennie Bible

Many Thanks

I want to thank Tom, my wonderful, good-looking supportive husband who always loves me. I want to thank my sons; Zach, Andrew & Phil who even though they tease me, love me & support my dreams. Thank you, Pastors Garry & Reba for teaching the Word & seeing the vision. Reba, you are a wonderful cheerleader and friend! To Carol for the grammar help and support. Thank you Kinda for your encouragement and example.

It has always been the desire of my heart to write books. God first puts those desires in our hearts. As we seek His will and plan for our lives those desires become ours. You honor me by reading my first book and I thank you. I believe God will bless you with revelation as you read.

Did you ever hear yourself say something that you knew was pregnant with meaning, but you didn't have the fullness of the words, at the time they came dripping off your tongue? That is what happened when at a wonderful women's

4

conference I spoke "quit sitting around on your ashes." The crowd erupted in laughter and I knew it to be a sentence I would need to remember. So when the revelations came for the book you hold in your hand, it had to be named "Quit Sitting Around On Your Ashes".

The conference where I was speaking was a WINGS conference. WINGS which stand for Women Impacting the Nations By God's Spirit is a marvelous conference held in Chelsea, Oklahoma, U.S.A. every year. I had long dreamed of being a

Key Note Speaker for this conference. I had
helped with registration, announcements, prayer,
attended faithfully every year and taught a few
seminars. It was a dream come true to speak on
the same platform with women I had long looked
up to as precious women leaders of the faith.

The founder of WINGS is my lovely friend and
Pastor Reba Wilson. Reba is a blessing to
everyone who comes in contact with her and I
thank her for her encouragement and leadership.

"Those things you thought were dead, I can bring to life. Give me those ashes and I will create more than you can ever dream or imagine".

The Significant Event

One bright and sunshiny day (I don't really know if it was bright or sunshiny that day but I always wanted to start a sentence with that phrase and it's my book so I just did it) as I was walking out to the yard, I saw the wheelbarrow. The wheelbarrow is old, grey with some concrete decorating it from a previous long past project, nothing special. It is very interesting to me that God uses ordinary, nothing special things and people to be involved in significant events. David was not even on his father's mind when Samuel

8

came looking for the next King of Israel. Peter was mouthy and denied the Lord when He needed him most. Paul persecuted Christians. Rahab was a harlot but we read about each one and the many ways God used the rather plain or even repulsive. It makes me smile when I am reminded by scripture that God uses plain and unlikely people for great and mighty acts because it gives me hope that He can use even me. Go ahead and smile, God can use you too! The wheelbarrow might even be considered repulsive; it is used by my husband to put the ashes in from the wood burning stove.

As I walked by the wheelbarrow loaded with last winter's ashes, a stalk of corn was growing. It was a miniature stalk with a tiny ear of corn. The little ear of corn was tinier than those canned miniature ears of corn you see in the store. It was an amazing sight and I smiled but I really didn't even slow my pace, after all I was busy with my "to do" list.

10

Quit Sitting Around on Your Ashes

I heard God say "take a picture". It wasn't
an audible voice but I knew it wasn't me. I am
not a person who takes pictures. In fact I have
three sons and the disparity in the number of
pictures for each son is appalling. Fortunately the
oldest, Zach and the youngest, Phil resemble.
Everyone knows the first born is well
photographed, it's a scientific fact. When the
baby, Phil couldn't find many pictures of himself I
told him some of the pictures of Zach were him. I
know it's bad but I didn't want the kid to think

he was adopted; I was just busy with three boys under six. The point I am making is I do not take many pictures.

I found my camera and took a few pictures. A few pictures, I am pretty sure this is a miracle corn growing out of ashes and I just take a few pictures! After I obeyed by taking the pictures, I heard God say" This is a spiritually significant event in your life". Don't miss my point; it was *after* I obeyed I heard why God asked me to do something I just never would have thought to do. In fact, it seemed silly to me.

Wow, that is a big deal! A significant spiritual event! I hesitate to tell you this but I must be truthful. I wish I could say I immediately stopped doing my "to do" list and studied, prayed, fasted and asked God what this spiritually significant event meant for my future. No, I just went on with my "to do" list and left the pictures in the camera.

One year later God, ever so gently reminded me of the corn growing out of the ashes. He highlighted Mark 4:26-28:

> And He was saying, "The kingdom of God is like a man who casts seed upon the soil: and he goes to bed at night and gets up by day, and the seed sprouts and grows—how, he himself does not know. The soil produces the crop by itself: first the blade, then the head, then the mature grain in the head. **NASB**

Quit Sitting Around on Your Ashes

Another year passed as I was preparing to speak at a women's conference God said this truth to me; *"Those things you thought were dead, I can bring to life. Give me those ashes and I will create more than you can ever dream or imagine"*.

God had a plan in that significant event of finding the corn stalk growing in the wheelbarrow filled with nothing but ashes.

Seeds Do What They Do

I am not sure how the corn seed got into the
wheelbarrow, maybe a bird dropped it or the
wind blew it, but nevertheless it landed in the
ashes. Seeds do what they are designed to do;
they reproduce what ever is in them.   The
Encarta Dictionary defines seed as the part that
contains the embryo and gives rise to a new
individual or something that is the source of a
significant change in outlook or action.

16

Quit Sitting Around on Your Ashes

When you look at a package of seeds there is always a nice picture of whatever the seed will become. If I want to plant some ruby red beets all I have to do is find the picture on the seed package. When I look at the seed itself it sure doesn't look like a beet but I trust that the manufacturer of the seed knows what is contained in the seed. A ruby red beet seed will not grow into a zucchini.

A seed can also be children or
descendants. We are the seed of Abraham. In
Genesis the twelfth chapter God tells Abraham
(his name was actually Abram at this time)

> "I will make you into a great nation, and I
> will bless you; I will make your name
> great, you will be a blessing. I will bless
> those who bless you, and whoever curses
> you I will curse; and all the peoples on
> earth will be blessed through you.
> **Genesis 12:2, 3 NIV**

18

If you have children and grandchildren they represent your seed.

> **You belong to Christ, so you are Abraham's descendants. You will inherit all of God's blessings because of the promise made to Abraham.**
>
> **Galatians 3:29 NCV**

In each of us is a seed. If you don't know what is in your seed you need to ask the manufacturer of the seed. In other words, ask God what you

are made of, what are His plans for you.

> **"For I know the plans I have for you,"**
>
> **declares the Lord, "plans to prosper you**
>
> **and not to harm you, plans to give you**
>
> **hope and a future " Jeremiah 29:11 NIV**

God does not want us ignorant of His plans for

us. He may not tell us every step of the way but

Quit Sitting Around on Your Ashes

He will let us know enough for the step we are on. We can trust that our Heavenly Father has great plans for us.

Take a moment right now and ask God what is in your seed?   What are the plans You (Father God) have for me?

Father God, who I am in you? What is my hope? What is my future? Well what did God tell you? What is in your seed?

Write it down: (really write it down, don't be ashamed or worried what someone might think, this is your book, write down what God said to you about your future!

_____

_____

_____

_____

_____

_____

_____

Quit Sitting Around on Your Ashes

Each seed is unique, as you are unique and special, different from every other person. There are some attributes that God says about us that we must all read and believe.

❖ You are the righteousness of God in Christ Jesus

2 Corinthians 5:21

❖ You are a royal priest (I can see your tiara)

1 Peter 2:9

❖ You are wonderfully made

   Psalms 139:14

❖ You have gifts

   1 Corinthians 12 (just read the whole chapter)

❖ You are loved by God **(John 3:16)**

The Bible is full of attributes of our seed. When we accept Christ as our Savior we become a new creation.

> **Therefore if anyone is in Christ, he is a new creation; the old is gone; the new has come. 2 Corinthians 5:17 NIV**

I have read that scripture and wondered "Lord when am I going to be different and new?" I was still reacting the same old way, losing my temper or saying evil words. Hey I thought I was a new creation! I learned it is our spirit that is new.

As we learn more about our wonderful savior and what is in our particular seed we start changing. The concept is a difficult one to learn, no one just automatically becomes a mature Christian. Our Spirit is new immediately but our mind and emotions must learn and develop through a process. So take a deep breath and give yourself some growing time!

An important point to note about seeds, as long as they stay in the package they will never grow. Seeds are dead. Seeds must be planted in order to produce what is in them.

Truly, Truly, I say to you, unless a grain of wheat falls into the earth and dies, it remains alone; but if it dies it bears much fruit. John 12:24 NASB

I believe this scripture tells us if we just remain interested in our own selfish thoughts we will not be the people God intended and has planned for us.

We will be like the seed that never looks like the picture on the package. So how do we get to that complete person? As the scripture states above when the grain of wheat (seed) falls into the ground and dies, it bears much fruit. We give ourselves to God's plan; we don't just do what we feel like. Forgive me if it sounds too easy or too hard, ___it is what it is___. The seed in you will not grow if it's not planted.

"Those things you thought
were dead, I can bring to
life. Give me those ashes
and I will create more than
you can ever dream or
imagine".

Ashes, Those Who Sit Around on Them

Ashes symbolize mourning; it's a sign of mourning. In Esther, Mordecai put on sackcloth and ashes and cried bitterly after he heard the decree that all the Jews would be killed. Mordecai was grief stricken with the death sentence on his people.

In 2 Samuel Tamar put ashes on her head after Amnon raped her. Amnon was her brother

30

and he should have had her best interest in mind but he raped her.

Then sent her away which was even worse for her. She spent the rest of her life a desolate woman. Tamar had her innocence stolen by someone who should have protected her.

Mordecai and Tamar went through some devastating experiences. You and I have gone through some stuff ourselves, loss of loved ones too early, senseless suicide, miscarriages, loss of dreams and relationships and many other painful experiences too numerous to mention and too horrible to write.

I have wanted to put ashes on my head many times. I know we don't actually put ashes on our head but sometimes I think it would just be easier. When people saw the ashes on our heads, they would know how horribly sad we are and how something had negatively affected us. We would not have to explain ourselves and hope for sympathy.

32

Quit Sitting Around on Your Ashes

I can hear the conversation now: Mary says to Judy "Did you see those ashes on Susie's forehead "she is getting divorced". Judy to Mary "What should we do for her?" "Should we each send a card or take her out for lunch?" "How can we help her? She has ashes on her head so you know she is mourning".

God does allow us to mourn; it is totally appropriate and needful for our healing. When my mother died, I was the only one in the room with her, I held her until she took her last breath.

I called the funeral home, made the phone calls to the people that need to be informed, made the arrangements and I even preached her funeral.

I was holding it together and being strong for everyone. Several weeks went by, I was at her home cleaning, picked up one of her bows (she would always wear huge bows in the back of her head, you would have had to know her!) and I burst into tears. How I missed my Mom! If I'd have had some ashes maybe someone would have known I was grieving maybe a little later than people usually do. I believe that is an example of delayed grieving, it happens. Without the "ashes" people don't understand why a person is sad, or not acting like they usually do. We all process a little differently.

Life is not a bowl of cherries (I think the bowl of cherries is suppose to be a good thing but I don't like cherries). Things happen that are yucky and disgusting. When we have losses we must have a time of mourning. We don't want to just "waller" (an Oklahoma word for lay around) around in our ashes, feeling sorry for ourselves. At some time we must stop sitting around on our ashes! We can develop an ashes mentality.

An ashes mentality is I am so sad, this bad thing happened to me and now it is completely defining me. The ashes are me.

Stop It! Get up and go wash the ashes off your face. God allows a time of mourning: I think it is forty days (don't quote me on that because there are several forty day time periods in the Bible).

36

Quit Sitting Around on Your Ashes

Nevertheless, God told Joshua this simple but profound statement:

"Moses my servant is dead: now therefore arise"... Joshua 1:2 NASB

Joshua was mourning the death of his leader and mentor; God allowed him some time but then He (God) said arise. Friend, (we are friends now right?) it's time to *quit sitting around on your ashes.* Say that last statement out loud, it will make you smile! I have sat around on my ashes and so have you but it's time to arise.

One of the great things I love about God is that He always has a plan. Remember in my significant event of the wheelbarrow, God said to me; " *Those things you thought were dead, I can bring to life. Give me those ashes and I will create more than you can ever dream or imagine".*

Answer these questions, what is dead in your life? Where are those ashes of God –given dreams? Do you desire to write songs of praise or poems to share with the hurting?

Quit Sitting Around on Your Ashes

Does a country burn in your heart? Do you long to rekindle some friendships? Do you desire to build a house, a ministry or a family? Do you long to go back to school? Do you want to learn to paint or play the accordion? As you read these questions do more questions enter your life? Do me a favor, (come on we are friends) take a few minutes or a few hours and just dream, remember your dreams.

Now write down those dreams that are in the

ashes:

_____

_____

_____

_____

_____

_____

_____

_____

_____

Quit Sitting Around on Your Ashes

Wow those are great dreams! Because we are friends I am going to share some of my dreams. Pardon me, they are a little dusty. I pulled them out of the ashes. As long I as could remember I wanted to write books. I am currently in the process of writing a book; if you are reading it then God just pulled one of those dreams out of the ashes, dusted it off and made it more than I could have dreamed possible. I did have to get up off my ashes and write it though, just saying.

I dream about making a difference in peoples' lives, of ministering to thousands. I also dream of learning to play the keyboard and painting beautiful pictures. I dream of having a beautiful, clean, organized house so I can invite folks over at the drop of a hat. The drop of a hat is a funny expression. It's not like I wear a hat to drop and what does that have to do with inviting people over.

42

Quit Sitting Around on Your Ashes

I just want to encourage you. I am sorry about your sad, heart wrenching experience and so is God. I hope you took time to mourn. Now if it has been long enough get off your ashes and give them to God! God will take those dusty dreams that lie in ashes and make more than you could ever imagine; but you need to give them to Him and arise just like Joshua did.

Joshua lost his mentor; he didn't think he could lead the people like Moses.

He missed Moses. God told him to cross the Jordan. God gave him the dream, the plan he had given Moses.

God told Joshua,

"Just as I have been with Moses, I will be with you; I will not fail you or forsake you. "

Joshua 1:5 NASB

Quit Sitting Around on Your Ashes

My dear friend, you may have been betrayed and mistreated by others but God will not fail you or forsake you. I am standing here in my cheerleader outfit (it does not fit like it did but the spirit is strong) yelling come on! Get up out of the ashes; give your dream to God! He is with you and will never forsake (abandon, dump, ditch, throw out, desert, walk out on, leave behind) you.

"Those things you thought were dead, I can bring to life. Give me those ashes and I will create more than you can ever dream or imagine".

46

Water Anyone?

Seeds are planted in soil but will not grow without water. I tested this theory; several of my plants have gone without water for days, maybe weeks. Without fail they all they wither and die. My husband says I forgot to water them, but I insist it was research.

Our dreams (seeds) are those plans deep within us and they need water. The water we need to use is words. Words are seeds in them selves; they can build up or tear down. We must learn to talk to ourselves, to water ourselves with words from our Creator. He put the dream in your heart so it can happen.

Write down the vision. I like to use pretty paper and pens or maybe design something on the computer when I am writing my dreams and visions. Confession time: I have a paper products fetish; I love to look at all different kinds of paper products. I can get so excited in an office supply

48

store that I need a cold shower. The variety of pens, pencils, paper, note cards, folders, binders, clipboards and legal pads is delightful and amazing but let me get back to the subject.

Write down to the detail what your dream looks like, sounds like, smells like (ok smells like might be a little off base). The point is writing it down so that you can read it over and over again. Read your dreams out loud. Water your dreams with the Word of God. Write down scripture that confirms and encourages your dream. After you have searched out the scriptures and written them with your dreams, begin to water them with your speaking. The following scriptures give us guidance. The truth is our words contain great power.

But I tell you that every careless word that people speak, they shall give an accounting for it in the Day of Judgment. For by your words you will be justified, and by your words you will be condemned."

Matthew 12:36, 37NASB

50

You will also decree a thing, and it will be established for you; and light will shine on your ways. Job 22:28 NASB

Death and life are in the power of the tongue, and those who love it will eat its fruit. Proverbs 18:21 NASB

You brood of vipers, how can you who are evil say anything good? For out of the overflow of the heart the mouth speaks. Matthew 12:34 NIV

Do not let this Book of the Law depart from your mouth; meditate on it day and night, so that you may be careful to do everything written in it. Then you will be prosperous and successful. Joshua 1:8

Water your dreams with the Word of God and your words. Surround yourself with people who believe in you and your dreams. Don't allow people to speak negative words into your life or your dream. Your dreams are you!

52

Quit Sitting Around on Your Ashes

Would you allow a person to speak horrible things to and about one of your children? Sally (Sally is a fictional person) comes over for tea (I always want to have people over for tea, I must do so sometime) and while you two are talking your precious son Marty (Marty is also fictional, but I do have an uncle Marty) comes into the tea room. Sally begins to say "Marty, you are a stupid little boy. You will probably not even complete grade school and your hair is too curly".

Any self respecting mother would throw Sally out on her assumption. As a matter of fact, I would not allow Sally to say something like that to one of my many dogs. Sally is never invited to tea again!

The example is extreme but we do listen to people berate our dreams. We must guard our dreams as beloved children! Protect them, nurture them and make decisions based on achieving your dreams and visions.

Quit Sitting Around on Your Ashes

I have a really sweet friend I will call her Kinda because that is her real name. Kinda is an author who wanted to pursue writing and speaking.

She had written a book but it was not yet published. She had a good job that paid her well; but she was not able to invest the time to go after her dreams. After much prayer, she quit her job. Many things happened and that is her story to tell but my point is she made decisions that allowed her to follow her dreams. At the time of this writing, her book is published; she's been on TV, had book signings to promote her book and is

also speaking about her passion. The moral of the

story; you should make decisions that lead to

your dreams.

"Those things you thought were dead, I can bring to life. Give me those ashes and I will create more than you can ever dream or imagine".

Wheelbarrows = Work

Wheelbarrow as defined by Encarta dictionary is a small cart used to transport things, usually in the form of an open container with a single wheel at the front and two handles at the back. When you see a wheelbarrow do you think of a nap? Or lunch? Or see a relaxing evening under the stars? No! When we see a wheelbarrow it represents work. It is going to be used to haul soil or remove weeds.

58

Quit Sitting Around on Your Ashes

Work is defined by the Encarta Dictionary as purposeful effort, the physical or mental effort directed at doing or making something. The wheelbarrow reminds us that if (I use if because we have a strong part to play in accomplishing our dreams) we are to see those God-given dreams come to fruition (I like that a word) we must do some work. We must get off our ashes, water the seed and do some work.

By the seventh day God had finished the work he had been doing; so on the seventh day he rested from all his work. Genesis 2:2 NIV

Do you see a man skilled in his work? He will serve before kings; he will not serve before obscure men. Proverbs 22:29 NIV

"I glorified You on the earth, having accomplished the work which You have given Me to do. John 17:4 NASB

Whatever you do, do your work heartily,

as for the Lord rather than for men,

Colossians 3:23 NASB

For even when we were with you, we

used to give you this order: if anyone is not

willing to work, then he is not to eat, either.

2 Thessalonians 3:10 NASB

I like to do the dishes because there is satisfaction of a job completed. First there is a sink filled with dirty and maybe smelly dishes if you wait too long. You take them out of the sink and stack them; I sort them by what should be in the dishwater last. The dirtiest, greasy pans would be last and the pretty glasses would be first. After cleaning the last dish, drying them (or letting them air dry which is my usual plan) you put them away and you just feel good a job well done. A sense of accomplishment fills your heart and your kitchen smells nice.

Work is a good feeling. Step by step you are accomplishing your goals toward your dream. Sometimes work is a four letter word. In my day you could get your mouth washed out for four-letter words, it can be unpleasant.

After many years of research in the area of work and it being unpleasant, I have some advice that I believe to be life changing.   Yes, get out your highlighter (another paper product that I failed to mention in my earlier true confession), my life changing advice regarding hard work and it being unpleasant is:

Get over it and get on with it!

I am saying that in my most loving, kind, and understanding way with a sweet smile and experience in my voice.

64

Quit Sitting Around on Your Ashes

We must just get over it, it's just hard sometimes. We must get on with it because we want to get that particular piece of work done.

I'm in my cheerleading outfit again, (picture me thin) come on, you will be so proud, happy, ecstatic (overjoyed, thrilled, elated, rapturous, jubilant) when you finish the work set before you. Remember when you are working, it's **Your Dream**. It might be helpful to go back to your dream that you wrote (on some lovely paper, I hope) and remember why you are working so hard. One of my dreams is to have a clean, organized home so that I can invite folks over at the drop of a hat. I can just dream about having a beautiful clean home, I can look in decorating magazines and plan my clean, beautiful home. It will never get done if I don't get off the couch and do it!

Some of the work will be done with the Holy Spirit. Let's replace the word work for renew or exchange. What God, Jesus and the Holy Spirit reveal, can be healed.

Quit Sitting Around on Your Ashes

Remember the wheelbarrow was full of ashes; dead, gray ashes but growing in the middle was a precious little stalk with a tiny little cob of corn. God can take ashes and grow corn.

You are reading this book (thank you for reading my book, it's an honor) probably because you have some "dead things" in your life you'd like to see brought to life. We must first admit that we have ashes. We must be willing to give those ashes to our Father. We must accept that

Jesus already paid the price for our healing and

we must work with the Holy Spirit for the new life

that God planned for us. Let's do so...

Out of the Ashes

Let's take a deep breath and admit we have been sitting in some ashes. Admit to yourself what in your life is in ashes. It may be a dream you have given up on, a relationship that is not functional, a deep pain from childhood or fill in the blank of why you are not living in the abundant life Jesus came to provide for you.

The thief comes only to steal and kill and destroy; I came that they may have life, and have *it* abundantly. John 10:10 NASB

Are you willing now to give those ashes to your heavenly Father? He can take those ashes, that which is dead and bring it to life?

He is our father in the sight of God, in whom he believed-the God who gives life to the dead and calls things that are not as though they were. Romans 4:17 NIV

Quit Sitting Around on Your Ashes

I have a dear friend named Mary who gave her ashes to her Heavenly Father. Mary was married for almost 28 years when her husband died of cancer. They had a wonderful family and loved each other so preciously. She was broken at the loss of her husband; she didn't understand why he was not healed of cancer. She missed him ferociously and she cried. Mary cried many, many tears! Through all her mourning Mary continued to praise God and put her trust in Him.

When we suffer loss we are entitled to a mourning period and Mary mourned. We spent many lunches together where she would cry. She went through a period of mourning and then she started to say "I'd like to have another husband." She gave her ashes to God, and eventually God sent her a new husband. I am happy to report I served as her bridesmaid. She was a beautiful bride and has a happy marriage.

Your ashes are safe with God. You can keep sitting around on them, but as long as you do God cannot fulfill His promise to you to make those things live again. So together now let us give those dead things in our life to the One who can help us.

 It will be helpful for you to picture yourself handing these ashes over to God, do it now. God is smiling; he so much wants to restore you to life.

 I'm so proud of you; you have taken a big step to your future! Celebrate, enjoy, pat yourself on the back as you have done something many people never do.

Quit Sitting Around on Your Ashes

Some people experience loss, a setback, or a problem and they just sit there on their ashes. They talk about what has happened to everyone who will listen. They play it over and over in their mind. They let that situation or situations control their life from that point on. So celebrate, you have stood up from your ashes and given those to your Father with the help of the Holy Spirit. You are made whole because of the blood of Jesus. Jesus willingly went to the cross so that we would be whole.

Quit Sitting Around on Your Ashes

But if the Spirit of him that raised up Jesus from the dead dwelleth in you, he that raised up Christ Jesus from the dead shall give life also to your mortal bodies through his Spirit that dwelleth in you. Romans 8:11 ASV

A word of caution here, sometimes you will be tempted to sit back on your ashes. You might get discouraged, the enemy will remind you of the situation, but you must remember those ashes have been given to God. Unfortunately, you may

---

have more than one situation in ashes and this process may have to be repeated. Jesus has already paid the price for your exchange of ashes to restoration.

The thief comes only in order to steal and kill and destroy. I came that they may have and enjoy life, and have it in abundance (to the full, till it overflows). I am the Good Shepherd. The Good Shepherd risks and lays down His (own) life for the sheep. John 10:10, 11 Amp

Quit Sitting Around on Your Ashes

Jesus willingly laid down His life so that we could have abundant life.

Don't be surprised that Satan (who is the enemy and father of lies) tries to steal your dreams, kill you physically and destroy your future. Jesus gave us this warning. Jesus has defeated our enemy and He came so we could have life, let Him turn your ashes into life.

Maybe you didn't give those ashes to Him at first time we did it, do it now. Maybe something else came to your memory, give it to Him now.

Go ahead, we will wait.

"Those things you thought were dead, I can bring to life. Give me those ashes and I will create more than you can ever dream or imagine".

My" To Do" List

I have never read in the Bible God saying" I am too busy" or maybe it would sound like "I am that I am too busy saith God". I have never heard a message preached that God is too busy to help His children. So why do we think we need to be so busy all the time? Why are we so busy we risk missing those brilliant moments of God's grace and wisdom? I almost missed a significant spiritual event because of my "to do" list!

Quit Sitting Around on Your Ashes

I am a list maker and I love to check things off I have completed. There is nothing wrong with that as long as I don't miss out on the special times of my life being too busy.

When I discovered the corn in the wheelbarrow, I just walked on by, have you ever done that? I mean notice something amazing or extraordinary and just dismiss it without giving it proper respect and reflection? God had to make me stop and take a picture. When I say God had to make me stop, He impressed on my mind.

I heard Him in my spirit instruct me to take a picture. The Bible says that we are His sheep and we hear His voice.

The gatekeeper opens the gate for him, and the sheep hear his voice and come to him. He calls his own sheep by name and leads them out. John 10:3 NLT

That is why the Holy Spirit says, "Today you must listen to his voice. Hebrews 3:7

Quit Sitting Around on Your Ashes

I obeyed after hearing the Lord tell me two or three times to take a picture. God also said "this is a spiritually significant event". You would think when I heard God tell me to take the picture; that it was a spiritually significant event, I would have spent some time in thought, reflection and meditation about this corn growing in ashes in a wheelbarrow. But no I went on about my business: my "to do" list.

Sometimes we are so busy doing stuff we don't even think about whether it is the plan

God has for us. We must think "is this the best use of our time?" We just write the list, do the task and check it off our list. We can get so busy we miss the significant events!

We miss or don't enjoy significant, important, major, momentous & huge events because we are busy doing things. I can tell you that I have no idea what was so important on my "to do" list that day. I am a big list maker and I love to write out my lists. Mostly I love to mark things off that I have done. Don't tell me I am the only one. You know you like to check things off your lists.

We must allow God to show us what is really important. I wish I could say that I spent hours and days after the event happened to hear from God as to why the corn growing was so important; but it was a year later before I even started the process. I was busy marking off tasks on my "to do" list.

I am not alone in my busyness, Martha was busy also. In Luke the tenth chapter we learn that Martha was busy preparing for Jesus. She was cooking and cleaning while her sister was sitting on the floor listening to Jesus.

I must admit I was with Martha all the way when she asked Jesus to tell Mary to come help her. What did Jesus say? He said Mary had chosen the good portion, meaning it was better to listen to Jesus than to scurry around serving.

Quit Sitting Around on Your Ashes

Let's not get so busy we miss out on what is important.

Our Impossible God

Corn growing from nothing but ashes in a wheelbarrow seems impossible to me. Healing a person from cancer is impossible for me. A rebellious child turning back to God and his family looks impossible. A person being set free from alcoholism or drugs, paying off a mountain of debt all seem impossible but our God is the God of the impossible!

Quit Sitting Around on Your Ashes

And looking at *them* Jesus said to them, "With people this is impossible, but with God all things are possible." Matthew 19:26 NASB

Throughout the Bible we see God doing all kinds of impossible. In Exodus 14 we read about the Israelites that had just been released from the captivity of Egypt. The enemy was coming after them and in front of them was the Red Sea; just in the knick of time God tells Moses to stretch his hand over the sea, God parts the sea. Those people walked across on dry ground with walls of water on each side. Amazing! Those water walls didn't stay up when the Egyptians came through. The Egyptians all perished.

The widow of Zarephath was planning to eat the last of her food with her son and then die but God sent Elijah. The little widow woman fixed Elijah a meal first and her flour and oil never went dry. An impossible miracle because the widow did first what God said to do.

Quit Sitting Around on Your Ashes

Daniel was sent to the lions den because he would not stop praying. Those lions were hungry and Daniel was supposed to be dinner but the next day he was still alive and well.

Jesus held a conference that had 4000 men; they didn't count the women and children so it could have been 10,000 people. The people were hungry, Jesus took five loaves of bread and a few fish and blessed it and fed them all, and they even had leftovers!

There are many stories of God performing impossible acts in the Bible. The earth we sit on is a miracle, God spoke and earth was formed.

God still is in the business of the impossible and what He has done for others He will do for you. Remember you gave Him your ashes!

"Those things you thought were dead, I can bring to life. Give me those ashes and I will create more than you can ever dream or imagine".

Wheelbarrow Wisdom

The lessons we have learned together from the corn growing out of ashes are many. We have learned that we are seeds, seeds become what they were always destined to be.

Ashes are an important part of life; we must acknowledge our painful events. We must mourn our heartaches for a time and then we must arise and move on. Ashes teach us what is

94

really important in our lives. We must not get

caught up in our pity party. Just like Joshua we

must move on into our promised land.

Water is vital to growth. Our water is the

word of God and the words of our own mouth.

We must water the seeds of our dreams and the

dreams of others along our way. We must use

the powerful words of wisdom of God.

Wheelbarrows are meant for work. We have

a part to play in our healing and achieving our

dreams.

We work together with the Holy Spirit to renew our minds and change into the dream we are destined. We must not get so busy with our "to-do" lists that we completely miss out on life's many blessings and God's direction. We must remember to be thankful for every miracle in our lives. Let's praise God for His mercy and grace. We have nothing except what God has given us. He has given us much, the world in fact!

Quit Sitting Around on Your Ashes

We serve an awesome God who has done a multitude of miracles and God is still in the impossible miracle business.

Remember we are all on the potter's wheel, somewhere in the process of becoming fully the destined seed. Dreams don't happen over night.

But we all, with unveiled face, beholding as in a mirror the glory of the Lord, are being transformed into the same image from glory to glory, just as from the Lord, the Spirit. 2 Corinthians 3:18 NASB

Let us give each other, our parents, our friends, our children a break! Let's quit knocking them off the potter's wheel before the appointed time. Let us encourage one another with our words.

> **Dear brothers and sisters, I close my letter with these last words: Rejoice. Change your ways.** Encourage **each other. Live in harmony and peace. Then the God of love and peace will be with you. 2 Corinthians 13:11 NLT**

"Those things you thought were dead, I can bring to life. Give me those ashes and I will create more than you can ever dream or imagine".

It has been my honor and pleasure to share a significant event from my life. I trust God will reveal to you His light on this matter. So what can I say, "Quit sitting around on Your Ashes!"

Blessings,

Jennie

Made in the USA
Charleston, SC
03 January 2011